Fostering Connection

WORKBOOK EDITION

Building
Social and Emotional Health
in Children and Teens

Dr. Tish Taylor

Fostering Connection: Building Social and Emotional Health in Children and Teens [Workbook]
by Dr. Tish Taylor

Copyright © 2023

Medical Disclaimer

This information is not intended as a substitute for the advice provided by your physician or other healthcare professional. Do not use the information in this book for diagnosing or treating a health problem or disease or prescribing medication or other treatment.

Artwork: Courtney Foat
Editor: Gail Fallen
Publishing and Design Services: MelindaMartin.me

ISBN: 978-0-9842725-3-2 (paperback)

Contents

INTRODUCTION

This is the companion workbook edition to my book *Fostering Connection: Building Social and Emotional Health in Children and Teens*. Its focus is to both support and expand upon the ideas and concepts in *Fostering Connection* as well as to help children and teens manage important relationships.

Connection and relationships with others is vitally important to our well-being. We naturally experience conflict or challenges within relationships, especially during childhood and adolescence. This is a time when children and teens are learning to communicate, negotiate different types of relationships, and manage their own emotions within those relationships. The lessons in this workbook illustrate various skills that increase self-awareness specific to communication and behaviors that directly impact interpersonal interactions. If you have or know a child who struggles with ADHD, behavioral challenges, or emotional regulation challenges, this workbook is for you. It provides valuable assistance to both adults and children by increasing emotional and social understanding, allowing children to interact in more positive ways. Even if a child does not have a particular behavioral challenge, concepts in this workbook will enhance their social-emotional knowledge base and help them to communicate more effectively in any situation.

The lessons and questions that follow have been created to help children and teens explore their behaviors through a variety of scenarios that illustrate interaction behaviors and patterns. The lessons also assist children and teens in formulating a plan to change and improve their interaction patterns. The ultimate goal is to help children regulate their problematic behavior and learn a number of skills and techniques that will foster positive connections with others.

This workbook is written for educators, parents, and mental health professionals. It is designed to be used following specific situations that are challenging for children or when working with a child or teen who is displaying behavior patterns that are disrupting their relationships. Created for use with children in middle to upper elementary school, middle school, and high school, this workbook is as practical as it is easy to use.

I wish you much happiness and connection!

Dr. Tish Taylor

Section 1

Situations

Use this section to help review a situation that has happened. This section highlights important behaviors that relate to connecting and disconnecting behaviors. Utilize one or multiple lessons as needed.

LESSON 1

Identify the Disconnector

FIGHTER

The Fighter enters a situation on guard, ready to defend their position or argue their point without seeing or considering the broader perspective. They only consider their feelings or thoughts, which are typically narrow in scope. This Disconnector often feels disappointed or frustrated.

DEFLECTOR

The Deflector is not willing or able to acknowledge their part in a situation. The Deflector blames others for the situation as well as for their own behavior. They find various reasons for their behavior, which others view as excuses. The Deflector presents as strong and willful. Deflectors may be reacting this way for different reasons: shame, feeling very insecure, or feeling upset with themselves on a deeper level.

The Insulator is unable to accept anyone's help in the moment. This Disconnector refuses to hear any constructive feedback or listen to what is being said to them, especially if it involves their behavior. The Insulator just wants to be left alone.

No Way shows up with a definitive attitude that communicates "I am not going to do what you say." The clear message is that this Disconnector rejects the other person's direction or request. No Way typically has a quick "no" response and can show a very mild reaction to intense refusals and behavior. This may include not stopping to consider the request or its consequences.

GRUMPMEISTER

The Grumpmeister shows up irritated, impatient, and annoyed. The Grumpmeister tends to pick on others and find fault in them or blame others for their feelings. This Disconnector brings all-around irritability to the situation, making interactions more difficult.

ONE WAY STREET

One-Way Street only sees things one way: their way. This Disconnector has difficulty moving away from their perspective. When other points of view are shared with One-Way Street, they typically respond with their own opinion, insight, or belief. This in turn does not allow for effective communication or understanding. It also diminishes the chance to problem-solve or collaborate.

Which Disconnector showed up in the situation? (There may be more than one.)

This is what (Disconnector name) did:

What did _____ do in this situation? What did they say or do that harmed the situation?

How did _____ change or affect the situation?

(If more than one Disconnector showed up, repeat these questions for that Disconnector.)

Notes

Notes

Identify the Disconnector's Behavior in Yourself

The Fighter

- Did you start or continue an argument?
- Did you hurt someone with your words or actions? Who?
- Did you try to get back at another person or seek revenge? Explain.
- Would someone else perceive your behaviors as bullying behaviors?

The Deflector

- What was your responsibility in the situation?
- Did you blame someone else or refuse to accept your responsibility?
- Did you argue instead of accept responsibility?

The Insulator

- Were you overwhelmed in the situation? How did you show it?
- Did you refuse to communicate?
- Did you ignore or pretend that you did not hear the other person?
- Did you not allow yourself to recover or start to feel better so that you could cope with the situation?

No Way

- Did you refuse to follow a direction or expectation?
- Did you ignore a direction or expectation?
- Did you put off or postpone a direction or expectation because you did not feel like doing it?

Grumpmeister

- Did you become irritated, grumpy, or agitated? How did you show it?
- Were you disrespectful to others?
- How do others describe your behavior?

One-Way Street

- Did you only listen to what you had to say? Did you listen to anyone else?
- Did you only consider your perspective?

Notes

LESSON 3

Self-Reflection

These are situations that involve other people and include specific feelings and thoughts. Feelings can be separated from thoughts. Think about each of these feelings in a situation that was difficult for you and circle those you experienced:

Disappointment	Insecurity	Fear
Frustration	Fatigue	Surprise
Anger	Anxiety	Hope
Sadness	Worry	Contentment
Jealousy	Overwhelm	Suspicion
Loneliness	Shyness	Irritation
Confusion	Guilt	Other:_____

List the feelings and record the thoughts that happened at the same time. Focus on those that helped the Disconnector(s) show up.

Example: *I felt frustrated when I wasn't picked to be quarterback at recess and thought that everyone was being unfair because I am better than the person they chose.*

List feelings	Record thoughts

Notes

Notes

Identify Your Values

Values are those qualities that are important to us or that represent who we want to be with others. Our values help us make decisions about our actions and our choices. Below you can circle your values or traits that are important to you and reflect how you want to act.

Circle your important values below:

Kindness	Trust	Assertiveness
Love	Safety	Playfulness
Compassion	Achievement	Self-Respect
Respect	Fun	Courage
Honesty	Curiosity	Flexibility
Generosity	Humor	Gratitude
Happiness	Fair-mindedness	Support
Leadership	Optimism	_____
Peace	Responsibility	_____
Knowledge	Wisdom	_____

Why are these values important to you?

What Connectors really match your values? Why?

Notes

_____

_____

_____

_____

_____

_____

_____

_____

_____

_____

_____

Notes

LESSON 5

Identify Connectors

FEELINGS MIND

You have feelings, thoughts, body sensations, and actions. They are all different things, but they often act together.

FEELINGS
INVESTIGATOR

You stop to understand your feelings, others' feelings, and why people are reacting the way they are in a situation.

HELPFUL COACH

You stop and think about the best choice in the situation, and you take a time-out to think when your emotions are overwhelming.

SHOES

You try to walk in another person's shoes by thinking about their perspective and feelings.

TWO-WAY STREET

Your perspective is different than others. Even so, you are willing to think about another person's thoughts and perspectives.

**CAPTAIN
COURAGEOUS**

You act courageously by admitting your feelings, your role in the situation, and working to help rebuild your relationships. Captain Courageous can assist in most situations. Captain Courageous is a wise and smart Connector that helps us lead with our values and our hearts.

MENDING
IN ACTION

You work to rebuild relationships. You allow yourself to care about others, the situation, and your values. Mending in Action can assist in situations when we have done something that is hurtful to others or to our relationship with others. Mending in Action cares. This Connector is humble, caring, and honest. Mending in Action is willing to admit when they are wrong and takes steps to heal and improve the situation and/or the relationships.

Which Connector could have helped the situation?

What would the Connector(s) have done in this situation? What would they have said or done that would have helped the situation?

How would this have changed or affected the situation?

Imagine how differently the situation would have turned out if the above Connector(s) had shown up.

(If you can think of more than one Connector who may have helped the situation, repeat these questions for that Connector.)

Notes

LESSON 6

Feelings Mind

FEELINGS MIND

You have feelings, thoughts, body sensations, and actions. They are all different things, but they often act together.

Think about the situation . . .

Identify your feelings:

Disappointment	Insecurity	Fear
Frustration	Fatigue	Surprise
Anger	Anxious	Hope
Sadness	Worry	Contentment
Jealousy	Overwhelm	Suspicion
Loneliness	Shyness	Irritation
Confusion	Guilt	Other:_____

Identify your body sensations:

Hot/Warm	Prickly	Jumpy
Jittery	Numb	Trembling
Nauseous	Sweaty	Twitchy
Shaky	Tight	Frantic
Tense	Breathless	Wobbly
Dizzy	Tired	Other: _____
Weak	Energized	
Frozen	Intense	

Share your thoughts in the situation:

Describe your actions in the situation:

Notes

_____

_____

_____

_____

_____

_____

_____

_____

_____

_____

_____

LESSON 7

Feelings Investigator

FEELINGS
INVESTIGATOR

You stop to understand your feelings, others' feelings, and why people are reacting the way they are in a situation.

Think about the situation . . .

Identify your feelings in the situation and circle all that apply:

Disappointment	Insecurity	Fear
Frustration	Fatigue	Surprise
Anger	Anxious	Hope
Sadness	Worry	Contentment
Jealousy	Overwhelm	Suspicion
Loneliness	Shyness	Irritation
Confusion	Guilt	Other:_____

What feelings did others likely have in the situation?

What would have been helpful behaviors in the situation?

How can you show care for yourself and others in the situation?

Notes

Notes

LESSON 8

Helpful Coach

You stop and think about the best choice in the situation, and you take a time-out to think when your emotions are overwhelming.

HELPFUL COACH

Think about the situation . . .

Stop and think when you feel these feelings (circle all that apply):

Disappointment	Insecurity	Fear
Frustration	Fatigue	Surprise
Anger	Anxious	Hope
Sadness	Worry	Contentment
Jealousy	Overwhelm	Suspicion
Loneliness	Shyness	Irritation
Confusion	Guilt	Other:_____

You need to stop and think _____ in these situations. Describe what you can think:

Where will you go if you need a break?

Who can help?

How will you make the situation better when you are really upset?

Notes

_____

_____

_____

_____

_____

_____

_____

_____

_____

_____

_____

_____

Notes

LESSON 9

Shoes

SHOES

You try to walk in another person's shoes by thinking about their perspective and feelings.

Think about the situation . . .

What do you understand about their feelings?

How are their feelings different than yours? Why?

Did you ask them about their feelings? What did they say?

Are their reactions different than yours? Why?

Notes

Notes

LESSON 10

Two-Way Street

TWO-WAY STREET

Your perspective is different than others. Even so, you are willing to think about another person's thoughts and perspectives.

Think about the situation . . .

Does the other person(s) think differently than you in the situation?

What opinions do they have?

What beliefs do they have?

Have you tried to understand them respectfully?

If you do not agree on everything, what *can* you agree on?

Notes

Notes

LESSON 11

Captain Courageous

CAPTAIN
COURAGEOUS

You act courageously by admitting your feelings, your role in the situation, and working to help rebuild your relationships. Captain Courageous can assist in most situations. Captain Courageous is a wise and smart Connector that helps us lead with our values and our hearts.

The following questions and answers are important to Captain Courageous:

What emotions are you feeling in the situation?

What is important to you about my relationship with

_____?

What values are important to you even if other people are not being kind or respectful?

Why should you want to honor your values even if others do not?

What can you say to show your values even if you are hurt or mad?

How can you be Captain Courageous and not accept disrespectful behavior from others?

How can you show others what is important to you in a way that respects yourself and others?

Often, identifying what is important to you can help you allow Captain Courageous to shine. Our anger, hurt, or disappointment toward another person can blur our ability to be Captain Courageous. It is helpful to identify the following:

What people are important to you?

What things or animals are important to you?

What events or things in your life are important to you?

What relationships are important to you?

These questions can help find ways to acknowledge the most important things above hurt and anger and help you to find *your* Captain Courageous.

Notes

Notes

LESSON 12

Mending in Action

MENDING
IN ACTION

You work to rebuild relationships. You allow yourself to care about others, the situation, and your values. Mending in Action can assist in situations when we have done something that is hurtful to others or to our relationship with others. Mending in Action cares. This Connector is humble, caring, and honest. Mending in Action is willing to admit when they are wrong and takes steps to heal and improve the situation and/or the relationships.

The following questions and answers are important to Mending in Action:

What is important to you about your relationship with

_____?

How was your relationship with _____
affected? Were they hurt?

How were you hurt?

What would make the situation better?

What can you do to make the situation better? Do you need to make an apology?

When and how will you do that?

Notes

Notes

Make a Plan

What would help this situation or what would have helped this situation?

What do you need to do now to mend the situation? Was someone else hurt?

Which Connector will be helpful?

Which Connector will show your values in this situation?

What will you say, do, and practice?

When will you do this?

Do you need any support or help? Describe.

Notes

Notes

Section II

Behavior Patterns

U se this section to help children and teens evaluate how they show up consistently or behave in ways that would be considered patterns. This section is meant to help them understand and reflect upon their patterns of behavior, including when Disconnector patterns occur. This includes understanding what may happen prior to Disconnector behaviors, assessing what thoughts and feelings occur that support Disconnector behaviors, and determining avenues for healthier patterns and change. Utilize one or multiple lessons as needed. (Adult assistance and/or coaching is typically required.)

Identify the Frequent Disconnectors

The Fighter enters a situation on guard, ready to defend their position or argue their point without seeing or considering the broader perspective. They only consider their feelings or thoughts, which are typically narrow in scope. This Disconnector often feels disappointed or frustrated.

DEFLECTOR

The Deflector is not willing or able to acknowledge their part in a situation. The Deflector blames others for the situation as well as for their own behavior. They find various reasons for their behavior, which others view as excuses. The Deflector presents as strong and willful. They may be reacting this way for different reasons: shame, feeling very insecure, or feeling upset with themselves on a deeper level.

INSULATOR

The Insulator is unable to accept anyone's help in the moment. This Disconnector refuses to hear any constructive feedback or listen to what is being said to them, especially if it involves their behavior. The Insulator just wants to be left alone.

No Way shows up with a definitive attitude that communicates "I am not going to do what you say." The clear message is that this Disconnector rejects the other person's direction or request. No Way typically has a quick "no" response and can show a very mild reaction to intense refusals and behavior. This may include not stopping to consider the request or its consequences.

The Grumpmeister shows up irritated, impatient, and annoyed. The Grumpmeister tends to pick on others and find fault in them or blame others for their feelings. This Disconnector brings all-around irritability to the situation, making interactions more difficult.

ONE WAY STREET

One-Way Street only sees things one way: their way. This Disconnector has difficulty moving away from their perspective. When other points of view are shared with One-Way Street, they typically respond with their own opinion, insight, or belief. This in turn does not allow for effective communication or understanding. It also diminishes the chance to problem-solve or collaborate.

Which Disconnector(s) show up the most for you in different situations?

What is a particular situation when at least one of these Disconnectors was present?

What other situations have been similar?

What often happens *before* the (Disconnector name) shows up? Do you tend to feel mad, hurt, sad, or upset about something? Is somebody doing something that annoys or upsets you?

What do you often *say* and *do* when this Disconnector shows up?

What do others do that may bring out this Disconnector in you? What happens around you? What happens inside of you? Think about this type of Disconnector situation and complete the chart below:

Example: *I know the Fighter shows up when I am mad and think my mom blames me for something that wasn't my fault. She never sees what my brother does and she blames me instead. When that happens, I am angry, frustrated, and sad that I am in trouble again. My body is hot and tight. Then I yell and slam my door.*

What feelings show up?		What thoughts show up?
Disappointment	Frustration	
Anger	Loneliness	
Sadness	Jealousy	
Loneliness	Confusion	
Insecurity	Fatigue	
Anxiety	Worry	
Overwhelm	Shyness	
Guilt	Fear	
Surprise	Hope	
Contentment	Suspicion	
Irritation	Other:_____	

What body sensations do you feel?		What actions or behaviors do you show?
Hot/Warm	Jittery	
Shaky	Tense	
Weak	Frozen	
Numb	Sweaty	
Breathless	Tired	
Intense	Jumpy	
Nauseous	Dizzy	
Prickly	Tight	
Energized	Trembling	
Twitchy	Frantic	
Wobbly	Other:_____	

Do you remember when this pattern may have started?

List any reasons why you think this Disconnector shows up.

Notes

_____

_____

_____

_____

_____

_____

_____

_____

_____

_____

LESSON 2

Defensiveness

Defensiveness is a common reaction when we try to protect or shield ourselves from someone else hurting us. We can show defensive behavior in order to avoid criticism or perceived criticism. Defensiveness can trigger Disconnector behaviors. It is important to think about how this may happen for you.

Example: Sarah enjoys collecting rocks at recess. She does not tend to play with most other classmates as she is not very interested in what they are doing and most are not interested in collecting rocks. A few kids have made comments to Sarah, such as, "Are you going to just sit on the ground again at recess? That is so weird." Sarah believes that many of her classmates think she is weird. So when someone mentions recess or their area of interest, Sarah tries to remove herself from the conversation. Sarah feels defensive about her interests and choices and others' reactions to them, so she starts avoiding any conversation on the topic. However, she now quickly pokes fun at others' interests. For example, she makes sarcastic comments when others mention playing basketball at recess. While deep down she does not care much about others playing basketball, she has developed a habit of putting it down.

Both types of reactions by Sarah—removing herself and making sarcastic comments—can be considered defense mechanisms. Both behaviors are Sarah's attempt to protect herself from further insults or mean comments that feel hurtful.

What *feelings* does a person have when they feel defensive? What *thoughts* might a person have when they feel defensive?

What is a situation when you have felt hurt by someone else? Did you feel defensive the next time that you were around them? What did you do to try and protect yourself and not feel hurt again?

Did you start to act defensive around others who may not have hurt you? Did they notice this pattern?

Are there particular people that you feel defensive around now? What defensive behaviors do you display? How do others react to these behaviors? Do others understand why you are displaying these behaviors?

Notes

Identify Your Values

Values are those qualities that are important to us or that represent who we want to be with others. Our values help us make decisions about our actions and our choices.

Below, you can circle your values—traits that are important to you and reflect how you want to act:

Kindness	Trust	Assertiveness
Love	Safety	Playfulness
Compassion	Achievement	Self-Respect
Respect	Fun	Courage
Honesty	Curiosity	Flexibility
Generosity	Humor	Gratitude
Happiness	Fairness	Support
Leadership	Optimism	_____
Peace	Responsibility	_____
Knowledge	Wisdom	_____

When do you act in ways that show your values to yourself and others?

What are some moments when you act in ways that do not match your values?

What could you do differently in those moments so that you could better reflect your values?

Notes

LESSON 4

Identify the Healthy Connectors

FEELINGS MIND

You have feelings, thoughts, body sensations, and actions. They are all different things, but they often act together.

FEELINGS
INVESTIGATOR

You stop to understand your feelings, others' feelings, and why people are reacting the way they are in a situation.

HELPFUL COACH

You stop and think about the best choice in the situation, and you take a time-out to think when your emotions are overwhelming.

SHOES

You try to walk in another person's shoes by thinking about their perspective and feelings.

TWO-WAY STREET

Your perspective is different than others. Even so, you are willing to think about another person's thoughts and perspectives.

CAPTAIN COURAGEOUS

You act courageously by admitting your feelings, your role in the situation, and working to help rebuild your relationships. Captain Courageous can assist in most situations. Captain Courageous is a wise and smart Connector that helps us lead with our values and our hearts.

MENDING
IN ACTION

You work to rebuild relationships. You allow yourself to care about others, the situation, and your values. Mending in Action can assist in situations when we have done something that is hurtful to others or to our relationship with others. Mending in Action cares. This Connector is humble, caring, and honest. Mending in Action is willing to admit when they are wrong and takes steps to heal and improve the situation and/or the relationships.

Which Connector(s) would help you feel better, happier, or more content?

Think about what this Connector would do in situations where you feel upset, mad, hurt, or sad. Imagine what a Connector would do. What would they say or do that would help you?

This is what (Connector name) would do:

This is what (Connector name) would say:

Imagine how you will feel when the above Connector(s) show up more often.

(If you can think of more than one Connector who would help you in different situations, repeat these questions for that Connector.)

Notes

Make a Plan Using Healthy Tools

(Note: This is a follow-up to Lesson 4.)

List the helpful Connector(s) you identified from Lesson 4:

Identify how the following *Healthy Tools* can help you:

- **Heart**: You can show your care and concern for others or yourself.

- **Eyes**: You can use consistent eye contact with a calm face.

- **Voice**: You can use a calm tone and respectful words.

- **Stop and Think**: You can stop before reacting with Disconnector behavior and think about a response that is respectful to yourself and others.

- **Thinking Brain**: You can recognize calm and considerate responses and not just your emotional response.

- **Breathe**: You can stop and take at least one deep breath before responding.

- **Listen**: You can listen to *all* of what the other person says, not just think about what you want to say back. You can repeat back to them what they have said so you are sure that you understand.

Explain how the Healthy Tools you identified will be used in situations where you feel upset, mad, hurt, or sad.

Notes

_____

_____

_____

_____

_____

_____

_____

_____

_____

_____

_____

Why Do the Connectors Disappear?

There are reasons why it is hard for the Connectors to show up in certain situations when it would be helpful if they did. We are going to explore why and how this happens for you.

Think about a situation when a Disconnector showed up, and identify which one. Why didn't a Connector show up instead? Consider the reasons below:

- You felt hurt or defensive.

- You were too mad.

- You thought that the other person didn't deserve it.

- You felt that you shouldn't have had to make an effort in that situation.

- You couldn't help it.

- You blamed them.

- Nobody was listening to you.

- Other:

Explain the situation and why a Disconnector showed up:

Why is behavior related to your values healthy for you, even when others hurt you or seem unfair to you?

When others do not appear to be kind or fair to you, how can your values and a healthy Connector show up for you? Even if you are not okay with what another person does, how can you react in ways that are more helpful than hurtful overall?

Notes

Replacing Disconnectors with Connectors

Think of a situation when one or more Disconnector(s) was present and it was not helpful. Describe what happened, including why the Disconnector(s) showed up in that situation.

Why did (Disconnector name) show up?

What were your behaviors?

What were your feelings?

What were your thoughts?

What were your body sensations?

What could you do instead of (see behaviors listed above) next time?

What Healthy Tools could you use?

How would you need to change your thoughts or attitudes toward yourself?

What support or help might you need?

Notes

ABOUT THE AUTHOR

DR. TISH TAYLOR

Dr. Tish Taylor is a licensed psychologist with a private practice in the greater Kansas City area. She has an established practice helping children, teens, and their families. She is also a licensed school psychologist and has years of experience working within school districts as a psychologist and coordinator of mental health services. In addition, Dr. Taylor is an adjunct professor who has taught child development for many years. She has previously written a book entitled *Parenting ADHD with Wisdom and Grace*.

Made in the USA
Monee, IL
13 September 2024

65720035R00067